MW01173352

Do You Want It?
No Fear
No Limits
No Excuses

"Jesus didn't die so we could be safe...He died, so we could be dangerous!!!"

ARE YOU READY TO BE DANGEROUS...???

Réal Andrews

Contents

Foreword

In my journey as a financial thought leader, I've discovered that success comes from following proven principles and taking direct action. For someone looking to find the results in their life they are not getting or are missing, they need to understand the power of five key principles: Discipline, Drive, Determination, Dedication, and Desire.

Growing up on a farm, Discipline was my constant companion, ingraining in me the truth that success is a product of persistent, dedicated effort. Day after day, whether tending to crops or managing daily chores, the unwavering routine and disciplined approach laid the foundation for my work ethic and achievements.

At Chevron, Drive became my inner voice, constantly pushing me to transcend the boundaries of comfort and reach for excellence. In corporate structures and conventional expectations, it was this relentless drive that fueled my ambition to innovate and excel beyond the ordinary.

Leaving my corporate job was more than just a career shift; it was a significant leap of Determination, driven by a crystal-clear vision of the goals I was passionate about achieving. In this moment of decisive action, fueled by a deep-seated belief in my vision and capabilities, I truly embraced the power of Determination to shape my destiny and forge a path that was uniquely mine.

Dedication served as my unwavering anchor during moments of doubt and uncertainty, a steadfast reminder of the goals that drove me - goals that extended beyond personal wealth accumulation to the broader vision of making financial success accessible to all. This commitment to a larger purpose helped me maintain focus, steering me through challenging times and reinforcing my resolve to create pathways for others to achieve their financial dreams.

Desire was the spark that drew others to me, turning my solitary dream into a shared mission of empowering others.

This isn't just a book to read; it's a manual for action designed to challenge and engage you in building your success. This book is a practical guide based on real-world experiences. It's about applying the Five D's in real life, not just learning about them. You'll find practical strategies and actionable steps that you can use immediately.

These pages are your guide to mastering these principles.

Approach them like a builder approaches a blueprint: with care, precision, and the belief that your efforts will create something lasting.

The road to success is challenging. It's full of challenges, but each one is an opportunity to apply the Five D's in a real and meaningful way. Your Discipline will be your foundation, your Drive will push you forward, your Determination will help you overcome obstacles, your Dedication will keep you focused, and your Desire will keep you motivated.

I invite you to not just read this book but to use it. To take these principles and put them into practice. This is your opportunity to use the Five D's to build a successful, meaningful life based on solid principles, not chance or destiny."

~Loral Langemeier

Introduction

I always seek moments of divine inspiration in the morning. I wanted to share this profound realization. At this stage in my life, every decision I make is guided by my faith in God. As I prepared to release my book, a pivotal moment came when Kimberly entered my life. She had the potential to help me launch my book, but it came with a significant cost that wasn't initially in our budget.

When I discussed this with my wife, who tends to be more practical while I'm the visionary, she pointed out that it wasn't financially feasible at that moment. In response, I turned to what I always do in such situations: prayer, quiet reflection, and worship. For me, significant events often occur in threes.

Remarkably, on the third day, my wife unexpectedly called me. She suggested that we should let fate decide whether this was meant to be, asking if God would show us a sign. She mentioned "residuals." Normally, when we receive residuals, they're for small amounts like 10 cents or $1.49. However, she sent me a picture of several residual checks, hinting at some upcoming excitement.

To my surprise, when I opened the first one, it was for $33, a significant number in my life. As I continued opening them, the amounts added up to cover not only Kimberly's fee but also unexpected expenses like a new car, bills, and groceries. This experience reinforced my belief that God's timing and provision are beyond remarkable; they are phenomenal.

This story emphasizes the importance of faith, prayer, and listening for divine guidance. Sometimes, when we pay attention and seek clarity, we discover what we are truly called to do and avoid heading in the wrong direction by listening to the wrong voices.

But there's more to the story. It's the realization that when we trust in God's plan, when we trust in the process, and when we believe that God has it under control, that's when we become truly unstoppable. When we hand over our worries, have faith, and exude confidence in God's power, we tap into our inner warrior. God is the ultimate warrior, and through Him, we become unstoppable. So, it's time for us to rise, show up, step up, speak up, and take action! Let's go to war, not alone, but with God by our side, because together, we are unbeatable.

The Blueprint for Achieving and Crushing Your Goals

As I stand at 60, reflecting on my journey through life, a profound realization has guided, empowered, and allowed me to achieve and crush my goals. It comes down to five simple yet mighty words: Discipline, Dedication, Drive, Determination, and Desire.

In this book, I want to share a blueprint, a roadmap, that you can follow to master these five words and transform your aspirations into accomplishments. These words have been my constant companions and guiding stars; they can be yours too.

Together, they form the foundation of success. This book is your guide to harnessing the power of these attributes to transform your life.

THE POWER OF DISCIPLINE

PROVERBS 12:1

CHAPTER 1

Chapter 1

The Power of Discipline

Proverbs 12:1

> *Whoever loves instruction loves knowledge. But he who hates correction is stupid.*

In the grand symphony of success, there exists a single note, a word of immense significance—a word that, when mastered, can transform dreams into reality. That word is Discipline.

Discipline is the foundational chord upon which the music of achievement is composed. The symphony conductor orchestrates your actions, the guiding star that lights the path to success.

As we embark on this journey to explore the five pillars of success: Discipline, Dedication, Drive, Determination, and Desire, we begin with Discipline for a reason.

Why discipline first? Because discipline is the keystone—the cornerstone of success. It's the word that, when etched into your daily life, has the potential to reshape your destiny. When you conquer discipline, you gain the key that unlocks the doors to success in every facet of your existence.

In this chapter, we delve into the art and science of discipline. We dissect its essence, explore its profound significance, and provide you with the tools and insights needed to master it. The journey may not always be easy, but it is an essential voyage. A voyage that, once embarked upon, will lead you to the shores of your wildest dreams.

So, let us begin with discipline, for in its mastery lies the promise of becoming a master of your destiny. Discipline is the first step that will take you beyond success and into a realm where you crush your goals, achieving greatness in all that you endeavor to do. Welcome to the journey.

Introduction to Discipline as The Foundation of Success

In life's grand tapestry, success is woven with threads like aspiration, ambition, and achievement. Yet, at its core, Discipline is the unifying force. It silently guides us through challenges and steers us towards our goals, making dreams real.

This book delves into the heart of discipline, exploring its role in success. Discover how to cultivate discipline, harness its power, and hear from those who've achieved greatness. Join us on this journey to unlock discipline's timeless wisdom and use it to shape your destiny. It's not a limitation but a liberation, enabling you to turn dreams into reality.

The Role of Discipline in Achieving Goals

Picture yourself on the brink of your dreams, gazing at your goals on the horizon. They're close yet seem out of reach. How do you bridge the gap? The answer: Discipline.

Discipline is your sturdy bridge from dreams to reality. It turns vague desires into concrete achievements. With it, goals are attainable.

We'll explore practical strategies to boost your discipline, whether you're starting from scratch or enhancing your existing discipline.

The Vital Role of Discipline in Goal Achievement

Imagine standing on the verge of your dreams, your goals within reach but still distant. How can you bridge this gap? The answer lies in discipline.

Discipline acts as your reliable bridge, turning vague desires into tangible achievements. Achieving your goals is only possible with it.

- **Consistency and Routine:** Discipline is a commitment to consistency. Incorporate your goals into your daily routine, making them non-negotiable, even in the face of distractions.

- **Defeating Procrastination:** Procrastination is your adversary, but discipline empowers you to resist it. Act, even when motivation wanes, and build momentum towards your goals.

- **Staying Resilient:** Challenges are inevitable on your journey, but discipline provides the resilience to overcome them. View setbacks as opportunities for growth and learning.

Practical Tips for Developing Discipline

Discipline, like any skill, can be developed and strengthened over time. We'll explore practical strategies to boost your discipline, whether you're starting from scratch or enhancing your existing discipline.

- **Set Clear Goals:** Define your objectives precisely. Specific goals are easier to commit to. For example, say, "run a marathon in six months" instead of "get in shape."

- **Create a Structured Routine:** Build a consistent daily or weekly routine that aligns with your goals. Stick to your schedule.

- **Prioritize Tasks:** Identify high-priority tasks that contribute significantly to your goals. Focus on these first, before less crucial matters.

- **Practice Time Management:** Utilize techniques like the Pomodoro Technique, which focuses on 25 minute stretches of work broken by 5 minute breaks, or time blocking to maximize productive hours. Minimize distractions.

- **Start Small, Gradually Increase Effort:** Begin with manageable steps to avoid being overwhelmed. As discipline grows, challenge yourself with more complex tasks.

- **Hold Yourself Accountable:** Use journals or goal-tracking apps to monitor progress. Self-accountability keeps you on track.

- **Find Your Motivation:** Connect with why your goals matter to you. Visualize the benefits of success.

- **Practice Self-Control:** Train yourself to delay gratification for long-term rewards.

- **Seek Support and Accountability:** Share goals with friends, mentors, or join supportive communities. Having accountability boosts motivation.

- **Learn from Setbacks:** Embrace setbacks as learning opportunities. Avoid self-criticism, and use failures as stepping stones.

- **Stay Physically and Mentally Healthy:** Prioritize sleep, exercise, and a balanced diet to maintain energy and focus.

- **Celebrate Small Wins:** Acknowledge and celebrate even minor achievements. Small victories fuel motivation.

- **Adapt and Evolve:** Be flexible and adjust your strategies as needed. Adaptation is crucial as you progress.

Success Leaves Trails

Here are some real-life examples of disciplined individuals:

Elon Musk: The CEO of SpaceX and Tesla is known for his incredible work ethic and pursuit of ambitious goals. He demonstrates exceptional discipline in managing multiple ventures while innovating relentlessly.

Angela Merkel: As the Chancellor of Germany for 16 years, Merkel displayed political discipline and earned global respect for her focused leadership.

Warren Buffett: A successful investor, Buffett's disciplined approach, long-term perspective, and principled decisions contributed to his wealth.

These individuals come from various backgrounds and pursuits, but they all share a common thread of unwavering discipline. Their stories demonstrate that discipline is a universal trait that can be harnessed to overcome obstacles, achieve greatness, and leave a lasting impact on the world.

Action Steps from The Millionaire Maker, Loral Langemeier for Discipline

Discipline is the bridge from your reality and your daily behavior to your dream and what it is that you really want. What is the biggest thing that helps anchor your discipline? They are your values and what you hold most important. Your values are what you live by; values are not your personality. Your values are the core of who you are in that you either have integrity or you don't. You either have a high value of health and you're driven to stay healthy, or you don't. There is a high intrinsic need to fulfill your values when you're living through your values. Knowing and anchoring your values to power your discipline is the only true approach to succeed.

What is an effective tool for maintaining and building discipline? Living by a calendar is extremely effective. Putting a daily, weekly, and monthly schedule together is one of the single, biggest factors for accomplishing goals. When you consistently block your days and time around your values, you'll be amazed at the success you're going to have because you have created an environment for your discipline to succeed.

*To Access Book Bonuses, go to: **www.DoYouWantItNow.com**

Action Step: A daily habit I can do/change to get closer to my goal is?

_____
_____
_____
_____
_____

Action Step: My new time blocking schedule is as follows: (Be specific, for example schedule in prayer time, family time, business etc.)

_____
_____
_____
_____
_____
_____
_____
_____
_____
_____
_____
_____
_____
_____
_____
_____
_____
_____

UNLEASHING THE POWER OF DRIVE

PHILIPPIANS 3:14

CHAPTER 2

Chapter 2

Unleashing the Power of Drive

Philippians 3:14

> *"I press toward the goal for the prize of the upward call of God in Christ Jesus."*

The word Drive is the next word in the blueprint for success. You know it's a mighty word. As you know, we can speak life and death over ourselves with the power of words. In this chapter, you'll get tools to develop a drive that could conquer nations.

The Essence of Drive

Drive is an unwavering commitment to excel, a relentless pursuit of greatness. It's fueled by passion, purpose, and the courage to overcome challenges.

Cultivating Your Inner Drive:

- **Passion and Purpose**: Find fuel for your Drive in your passions and sense of purpose.

- **Setting Compelling Goals:** Learn to set inspiring goals that keep your Drive alive.

- **Overcoming Fear:** Conquer fear and use it as a stepping stone to Drive.

- **Embracing Challenges**: View challenges as opportunities for growth.

- **Staying Motivated:** Discover techniques to maintain your inner fire.

Drive in Action: Explore real-life examples of individuals who harnessed their inner Drive for remarkable feats. By the end of this chapter, you'll have the tools to cultivate a drive so powerful that it propels you through any challenge. Let's embark on this journey to unlock the extraordinary power of drive and break through the limits of what you believe is possible.

Exploring What Drive Means and Why It's Crucial

In the tapestry of success, "drive" stands out as a vital thread. This chapter explores the essence of drive and why it's pivotal to success.

Defining Drive: Drive is the inner force that propels us with relentless determination. It fuels ambition, commitment to goals, and resilience in adversity.

The Crucial Role of Drive:

- Motivation's Core: Drive sustains motivation through ups and downs, reigniting determination after setbacks.

- Catalyst for Action: It transforms intentions into actions, propelling us to take steps toward our goals.

- Overcoming Challenges: Drive empowers us to confront obstacles, viewing them as growth opportunities.

- Consistency and Resilience: It supports character and resilience, which are essential for success.

- Bridge from Vision to Reality: Drive turns dreams into accomplishments, bridging the gap.

- Fuel for Ambition: It nurtures ambition, driving us to aim higher and push boundaries.

- Inner Strength: Drive is a reservoir of inner strength in moments of doubt or fatigue.

- Success Differentiator: It distinguishes those who achieve remarkable success from the ordinary.

Drive isn't fleeting; it's an inner energy source. Discover and nurture your drive for relentless pursuit and boundless achievement.

Discovering and Cultivating Your Drive

Drive is not a one-size-fits-all concept; it's deeply personal and unique to each individual. In this chapter, we embark on a journey of self-discovery to uncover your drive and learn how to cultivate it into a potent force that propels you toward your goals.

Self-Reflection: The First Step

Know Thyself

Self-awareness is the foundation for discovering your drive. Reflect on your values, passions, and aspirations. What truly matters to you? What stirs your inner fire? Your drive often lies in alignment with these core elements of your being.

Past Successes and Failures

Examine your past accomplishments and setbacks. What motivated you to succeed in those moments? What held you back in times of failure? These experiences can reveal valuable insights about your sources of drive.

Setting Personal Goals: The North Star

Set Compelling Goals:

Drive flourishes in the pursuit of meaningful objectives. Set clear and inspiring goals that resonate with your values and aspirations. Whether career milestones, personal achievements, or contributions to a cause, these goals will be your guiding stars.

Prioritize Goals

Focus on your most significant goals for a precise and dedicated drive.

Cultivating Your Drive: The Nurturing Process

- **Continuous Learning:** Embrace curiosity and a hunger for knowledge.

- **Surround Yourself with Inspiration:** Seek out role models and mentors.

- **Stay Resilient:** Embrace failure as a teacher and celebrate setbacks as stepping stones.

- **Celebrate Small Wins:** Acknowledge and celebrate achievements, even small ones.

- **Maintain Balance:** Balance ambition with self-care for sustained motivation.

Consistent Action: The Expression of Drive

1. **Create a Routine:** Establish a daily routine aligned with your goals.

2. **Keep a Drive Journal:** Document your journey to track progress and adjust your course.

3. **Visualize Success:** Use visualization to make your objectives feel attainable.

Your personal drive is a dynamic force within you, waiting to be harnessed. By embarking on this journey of self-discovery and nurturing your drive through thoughtful goals and consistent action, you'll find your inner fire burning brighter than ever before. In the chapters ahead, we'll explore how to maintain and fuel your drive, even in the face of challenges and setbacks, helping you reach unprecedented heights of achievement.

Overcoming Obstacles and Staying Motivated

Any journey will inevitably encounter obstacles, especially if you are motivated. We will explore strategies to overcome challenges and maintain unwavering motivation in adversity.

Understanding Obstacles

1. **Identify Your Challenges:** Recognize what stands in your way, whether it's external factors or self-doubt.

2. **Shift Your Perspective:** View obstacles as opportunities for growth and character building.

Strategies for Overcoming Obstacles

- **Break it Down:** Divide large obstacles into smaller, manageable tasks to track progress.

- **Seek Solutions:** Approach obstacles with a problem-solving mindset and be willing to pivot.

- **Embrace Resilience:** Remind yourself of your larger goals when faced with setbacks and keep moving forward.

- **Learn from Setbacks:** Analyze what went wrong, adjust your approach, and apply lessons to future challenges.

Maintaining Motivation

- **Visualize Success:** Revisit your goals and vividly imagine the rewards of achievement.

- **Celebrate Small Wins:** Acknowledge and reward yourself for achievements, no matter how small.

- **Stay Connected to Your Why:** Reconnect with the reasons driving your pursuit.

- **Seek Support:** Share your challenges and aspirations with trusted individuals for encouragement and advice.

- **Stay Inspired:** Continuously seek inspiration from various sources aligned with your goals.

- **Maintain a Growth Mindset:** Embrace the belief that challenges foster growth and resilience.

Perseverance as a Way of Life

Overcoming obstacles and staying motivated are ongoing processes integral to the journey of success. The drive is about confronting challenges head-on with unwavering determination. Approach obstacles as stepping stones, not barriers. You'll overcome challenges and emerge more substantial and driven by maintaining motivation through visualization, celebrating wins, seeking support, and embracing a growth mindset. In upcoming chapters, we'll delve deeper into the qualities of driven individuals and explore the stories of those who've overcome immense obstacles on their path to success.

Success Leaves Trails

Stories of Drive Turned into Success

Real-life stories of individuals who transformed their unwavering drive into remarkable success serve as powerful inspiration. We'll explore the stories of five extraordinary people who achieved greatness through their determination.

1. Stephen Hawking: A Brilliant Mind Against All Odds Physicist. Stephen Hawking's unyielding drive to understand the universe persisted despite his battle with ALS. He continued groundbreaking research and communication of ideas, defying physical limitations.

2. Elon Musk: Revolutionizing Space Travel. Elon Musk's relentless drive led to the founding of SpaceX, despite numerous setbacks. His vision resulted in the successful launch of the Falcon 1 rocket, marking a historic milestone in private space exploration.

3.**Oprah Winfrey**: **From Humble Beginnings to Media Mogul** Oprah Winfrey's determination to break barriers in the media industry created an empire, including "The Oprah Winfrey Show," OWN, and more. Her story exemplifies the power of drive.

4. **Michael Jordan: The Epitome of Determination** Basketball Legend. Michael Jordan's unmatched drive to succeed propelled him through setbacks. His work ethic and ability to thrive under pressure made him an iconic figure in sports.

These individuals, from diverse backgrounds, share an unwavering drive that propelled them to greatness. Their stories remind us that drive is a living force that can lead to extraordinary achievements. Drawing inspiration from their journeys, we can amplify our own drive and strive for remarkable success in our unique ways.

Action Steps from The Millionaire Maker, Loral Langemeier for Drive

Drive is a deeply intrinsic value, yet it comes from the idea of that personal mission beyond yourself. Drive is what will keep your mission in front of you and at all costs. As long as it is legal and ethical, you should use your inner drive to go and achieve or accomplish that personal mission. You will inevitably encounter obstacles as you're driving towards your goal. When you are nimble, agile, and creative in overcoming these obstacles, you can rest assured that you know you're going to complete your mission. When you find and work with a mentor or coach, they will help you maintain a plan of action and build your discipline, and you will start to become an all-but-unstoppable force.

*To Access Book Bonuses, go to: **www.DoYouWantItNow.com**

Action Step: What fuels my drive?

_____
_____
_____
_____
_____
_____
_____
_____

Action Step: My MISSION in this life is?

_____
_____
_____
_____
_____
_____
_____
_____

MASTERING
DETERMINATION

3

CHAPTER

Chapter 3

Mastering Determination

Philippians 4:13

> *I can do all this through him who gives me strength.*

Determination, often overshadowed by flashier traits, plays a unique and vital role in success. In this chapter, we explore determination—the third element in our blueprint for success—and uncover why it's a silent hero worth recognizing.

Determination is the unwavering commitment to persist, the inner strength that guides us through challenges. It sets achievers apart from mere dreamers. In a world of quick fixes, determination is the steady force that propels us on long, challenging journeys.

Why Determination Matters

In a world of instant gratification, determination is the silent, persistent force that carries us through tough journeys. In this chapter, we'll cover:

- **The Tenacity of Determination:** How it builds resilience and helps us rebound from setbacks.

- **The Role of Grit:** Grit, born from passion and perseverance, fuels determination.

- **Navigating Obstacles:** Determination turns obstacles into stepping stones.

- **The Power of a Growth Mindset:** Techniques to maintain determination through ups and downs.

- **Determination in Action:** Real-life stories of those who embody determination in their pursuit of success.

By the end, you'll understand why determination is the unsung hero in our blueprint for success. The grit that turns dreams into reality, the unwavering resolve that keeps us on track when others waver. Let's shine a light on the power of determination and give it the recognition it deserves on our path to success.

Strengthening Your Determination

Now that we grasp the critical role determination plays in your path to success, let's dive into practical strategies to bolster this essential quality. Whether starting from scratch or looking to enhance your determination further, these strategies will be your guide.

1. **Define Your "Why" Clearly:**

   o   Your "why" fuels your determination. Clearly define the reasons behind your goals to strengthen your determination.

2. **Set SMART Goals:**

   o   Specific, Measurable, Achievable, Relevant, Time-bound goals provide clarity and benchmarks to enhance determination.

3. **Break Goals into Manageable Steps:**

   o   Divide large goals into achievable steps. Completing each step fuels your determination for the next.

4. **Cultivate a Growth Mindset:**

   o   See challenges as opportunities for growth. This mindset shift boosts determination by turning setbacks into stepping stones.

5. Stay Inspired:

- Seek inspiration from books, documentaries, and determined individuals. Their journeys can reignite your determination.

6. Develop Resilience:

- Accept setbacks as part of the journey. Bounce back stronger and more determined after each setback.

7. Create a Supportive Environment:

- Surround yourself with people who support your goals. A strong support network boosts determination.

8. Practice Self-Discipline:

- Habits and routines reinforce commitment to your goals. Consistent effort fosters unwavering determination.

9. **Focus on the Process, Not Just the Outcome:**

   - o Embrace the journey and find joy in daily actions that lead to your goals.

10. **Visualize Success:**

   - o Regularly visualize achieving your goals. This mental rehearsal makes your objectives feel attainable.

11. **Keep a Determination Journal:**

   - o Document thoughts and experiences related to determination. Use it for motivation during challenging times.

12. **Accept Discomfort:**

   - o Determination often means leaving your comfort zone. Embrace discomfort as a sign of growth.

13. **Celebrate Achievements:**

   o Acknowledge and celebrate both big and small achievements. Recognizing progress reinforces determination.

14. **Maintain Patience:**

   o Trust the process and stay patient. Persistence over time is a testament to unwavering determination.

Remember, determination is a quality you can develop and refine. Consistently applying these strategies will turn it into a powerful force driving you towards success. In upcoming chapters, we'll explore how to harness this determination to achieve ambitious goals in various aspects of your life.

Dealing with Setbacks and Maintaining Resolve

Setbacks are inevitable in any journey; how you respond to them can make or break your determination. This chapter will explore strategies for handling setbacks and preserving your unwavering resolve in the face of adversity.

Understanding Setbacks

- **Accept the Inevitability of Setbacks:**
    - Setbacks are not indicators of failure; they are part of the path to success. Accepting this reality can help you approach setbacks with a healthier perspective.
- **Dissect the Setback:**
    - When faced with a setback, take time to analyze what went wrong. Identify the specific factors or actions that contributed to the setback. Understanding the root causes is crucial for making informed adjustments.

Strategies for Maintaining Resolve During Setbacks

- **Stay Committed to Your "Why":**
    - Your initial motivation and the reasons behind your goals remain as valid during setbacks as during moments of progress. Remind yourself of your "why" to rekindle your determination.

- **Refocus on Short-Term Goals:**
  - While long-term goals are essential, during setbacks, concentrate on short-term objectives. Achieving smaller milestones can rebuild your confidence and determination.

- **Lean on Your Support Network:**
  - Reach out to your support network, whether it's friends, family, mentors, or a coach. Sharing your challenges and seeking advice can provide valuable perspective and emotional support.

- **Adapt and Adjust:**
  - Setbacks often require adjustments to your approach. Be flexible and open to change. Adaptation is a sign of strength, not weakness.

- **Maintain a Growth Mindset:**
  - View setbacks as opportunities for growth and learning. Each obstacle can provide valuable lessons that enhance your determination.

- **Visualize Your Comeback:**
    - Use the power of visualization to imagine yourself overcoming the setback and getting back on track. This mental imagery can reignite your determination.
- **Practice Self-Compassion:**
    - Be kind to yourself during setbacks. Self-criticism can erode determination, whereas self-compassion can help you bounce back with renewed resolve.

The Resolve to Keep Moving Forward

Setbacks do not define your journey; your response to them does. The most determined individuals can weather setbacks gracefully, adapt their strategies, and emerge from challenges stronger.

Remember that maintaining your resolve during setbacks is a testament to your determination. It's a sign that you are committed to your goals, no matter the obstacles that arise. By embracing setbacks as opportunities for growth and resilience, you'll find that your determination remains unshakable on your path to success. In the forthcoming chapters, we'll explore how to use this resolve to achieve your greatest ambitions in specific areas of your life.

Success Leaves Trails

Inspirational Stories of Unwavering Determination of Champions who never gave up. We will delve into the stories of remarkable individuals who faced seemingly insurmountable challenges but refused to surrender. Their unwavering determination and resilience serve as beacons of inspiration for anyone striving to overcome adversity and achieve their goals.

1. Nelson Mandela: A Triumph of Resolve

Nelson Mandela spent 27 years imprisoned for his anti-apartheid activism in South Africa. Despite the harsh conditions and prolonged captivity, his unwavering determination to end apartheid never wavered. He continued his fight for justice and equality upon his release, ultimately becoming South Africa's first democratically elected president. His story demonstrates the power of determination to overcome even the most formidable obstacles.

2. Nick Vujicic: Triumph Over Physical Limitations

Nick Vujicic was born without limbs, facing profound physical challenges. However, he refused to be defined by his limitations. Through determination and an unshakable positive attitude, he became a motivational speaker, author, and advocate for people with disabilities. Nick's story inspires us to transcend adversity with unwavering determination and a resilient spirit.

3. Bethany Hamilton - Surfing Against the Odds:

At 13, Bethany Hamilton lost her arm in a shark attack while surfing. Rather than giving up her passion, her determination to surf again pushed her to adapt and persevere. She returned to the waves and became a professional surfer and an inspiration to countless aspiring athletes.

4. Helen Keller - Overcoming Silence and Darkness:

Helen Keller, born deaf and blind, could have succumbed to isolation and despair. Instead, her relentless determination to communicate and learn drove her to achieve remarkable feats. With the help of her teacher, Anne Sullivan, Keller learned to speak, read, and write, becoming a renowned author and advocate for people with disabilities.

Action Steps from The Millionaire Maker, Loral Langemeier for Determination

Determination is different from dedication. Determination shows itself when challenges arrive and all you first see are obstacles in front of you. Someone who is determined will back up and get curious about their options, solutions, and possible actions. I cannot tell you enough to get the right mentor and community around you to support you for your determination.

Determination also comes from not just letting people know what you want but sharing your goals out loud with them. Share your goals. Share your dreams. Get support from mentors or coaches, from mastermind teams, or others who will really support you through these obstacles as you achieve your goals.

A great way to stay determined is to put visual cues about your goals around you to keep those goals present while reminding yourself that you are worth it. You deserve it, and the people that you want to serve deserve you to have the determination to get to your goal.

*To Access Book Bonuses, go to: **www.DoYouWantItNow.com**

Action Step: How have I shown determination in overcoming obstacles I have faced?

_____

_____

_____

_____

_____

_____

Action Step: What Mentors/Coaches could I learn from?

_____

_____

_____

_____

_____

_____

Action Step: My top 3 goals are:

_____

_____

_____

_____

_____

_____

THE ART OF DEDICATION

COLOSSIANS 3:23

CHAPTER 4

Chapter 4

The Art of Dedication

Colossians 3:23

> *Whatever you do, work at it with all your heart, as working for the Lord, not for human masters.*

Long-term success results from unwavering dedication, persistent effort, and a commitment to the journey. In this chapter, we will delve into the significance of dedication and how it sustains your pursuit of long-term goals, impacting your path to success.

The Essence of Long-Term Success

- **A Marathon, Not a Sprint:** Long-term success is a lifelong journey, not a fleeting endeavor. Dedication is the guiding light that keeps you steadfast, no matter the challenges or triumphs.

- **Consistency Over Time:** Dedication underscores the importance of consistency, prolonged effort. It empowers you to stay engaged, even when immediate results are elusive.

Dedication as Your North Star

- **Navigating Uncertainty:** Long-term goals often come with uncertainties and setbacks. Dedication serves as your compass, helping you navigate the fog of uncertainty and stay on course.

- **Overcoming Plateaus:** Plateaus and slow progress are standard for long-term success. Dedication motivates you to persist through these plateaus, knowing your efforts will bear fruit.

- **Resisting Short-Term Temptations:** Short-term distractions can divert you from your long-term goals. Dedication provides the strength to resist these temptations and focus on what truly matters.

The Legacy of Dedication

- **Achieving Mastery:** Dedication is the gateway to mastery. It allows you to refine your skills, deepen your knowledge, and excel in your chosen field over time.

- **Inspiring Others:** Your dedication to long-term goals can inspire those around you, showcasing the power of unwavering determination as a beacon of possibility.

- **Personal Growth and Fulfillment:** The journey towards long-term success is as much about personal growth and fulfilment as the result. Dedication leads to self-discovery and profound accomplishment.

Dedication in Action:

Real-Life Examples

- **Warren Buffett:** Warren Buffett's dedication to investing is legendary, leading to his status as one of the world's most successful investors through his unwavering commitment to his principles.

- **Angela Merkel:** Angela Merkel's dedication to her political career made her Germany's first female Chancellor, exemplifying patient and steady leadership.

- **Leonardo da Vinci:** Leonardo da Vinci's dedication to art and science resulted in timeless masterpieces and groundbreaking scientific discoveries, inspiring generations.

The Unyielding Force of Dedication

Dedication to pursuing long-term success is not a fleeting emotion; it's a persistent force within you. It lights the path to your goals and guides your journey. Recognizing the profound significance of dedication will empower you to face challenges, overcome setbacks, and reach unparalleled heights of success. In this chapter, we'll explore how to nurture and fortify your dedication, ensuring it remains a steadfast companion on your path to long-term greatness.

Cultivating Dedication Through Habits and Routines

Dedication is not solely about bursts of motivation; but is often forged through consistent habits and routines. We will dive into cultivating faith by integrating purposeful practices and patterns into your daily life.

The Power of Consistency

Habits as Building Blocks: Dedication is not an isolated trait but a product of consistent actions.

Habits form the foundation of dedication, shaping your daily behaviors and reinforcing your commitment to long-term goals.

Routines as Anchors: Routines provide structure and stability to your days. They create a dependable framework for cultivating dedication by consistently allocating time and energy to your goals.

Strategies for Cultivating Dedication Through Habits and Routines

Set Clear Intentions: Define your goals with precision and clarity. Knowing what you're working toward is essential for designing habits and routines that align with your aspirations. Start Small and Build Momentum: Begin with manageable habits and routines. Gradually increase their complexity and intensity as you build dedication over time. Small victories fuel the desire to do more.

Be Consistent: Dedication thrives on consistency. Commit to your chosen habits and routines daily or at designated intervals. Consistency reinforces your determination.

Embrace Accountability: Share your goals and routines with a trusted friend, mentor, or coach. Accountability partners can help you stay committed and track your progress.

Review and Adjust: Regularly evaluate your habits and routines to ensure they remain effective. Make adjustments as needed to stay aligned with your goals and aspirations.

Sample Dedication-Boosting Habits and Routines

Morning Rituals: Start your day with a routine that primes you for dedication. This may include meditation, goal setting, or physical exercise to invigorate your mindset.

Focus Blocks: Dedicate specific time blocks for focused work on your most important tasks. Eliminate distractions during these periods to maximize productivity.

Daily Reflection: End each day with a moment of reflection, reviewing your accomplishments, setbacks, and progress toward your long-term goals. Use this reflection to strengthen your dedication.

Real-Life Examples of Dedication Through Habits and Routines

Benjamin Franklin:

Benjamin Franklin meticulously structured his day around a routine that included learning, work, and reflection time. This dedication to a daily routine significantly influenced his success as a polymath and inventor.

Maya Angelou: Maya Angelou maintained a steadfast writing routine, checking into a hotel room to write and removing distractions. This routine helped her produce her iconic works.

Jerry Seinfeld: Comedian Jerry Seinfeld famously employed a "Don't Break the Chain" method to maintain his dedication to writing jokes. He marked an X on a calendar for each day he completed his writing task, creating a visual chain he was determined not to break.

The Transformative Power of Dedication

Cultivating dedication through habits and routines is a deliberate and transformative process. You build the foundation for unwavering commitment to your long-term goals by embedding purposeful actions into your daily life. Dedication becomes second nature, guiding you toward success and fulfillment. In the upcoming chapter, we'll explore how faith can be applied to specific aspects of your life, amplifying your achievements and propelling you toward your greatest aspirations.

Balancing Dedication with Other Life Priorities

Dedication to your goals is commendable, but it should harmonize with other essential aspects of life. Here we explore balancing faith with key life priorities, ensuring that your commitment enhances your overall well-being.

The Multifaceted Nature of Life Priorities

- **Family and Relationships:** Family bonds and relationships are foundational to well-being. Balancing dedication involves nurturing these connections and being present for loved ones.

- **Health and Well-being:** Physical and mental health are paramount. Dedication shouldn't compromise self-care. Balance means making time for exercise, nutrition, and stress management.

- **Work and Career:** Professional growth is vital, but it must coexist with other priorities. Balancing ensures that your career commitment complements your life satisfaction.

- **Personal Growth and Fulfillment:** Dedication to personal growth and passions is essential. These pursuits provide purpose and should not be overshadowed by single-minded dedication.

Strategies for Balancing Dedication with Life Priorities

- **Set Clear Boundaries:** Establish boundaries between dedicated work and other priorities. Respect these boundaries to maintain balance.

- **Prioritize Effectively**: Use time management techniques to prioritize tasks and goals. Ensure that important but non-urgent life priorities receive attention alongside dedicated pursuits.

- **Delegate and Seek Support:** Delegate tasks and seek support in both professional and personal life. It eases the burden of dedication, creating space for other priorities.

- **Practice Mindfulness:** Mindfulness practices help you stay present and fully engaged in tasks, whether it's dedicated work or quality time with loved ones.

Real-Life Examples of Balancing Dedication and Life Priorities

1. Oprah Winfrey:

Oprah balances her career with philanthropy, family, and self-care. She advocates for wellness and mindfulness while maintaining a highly successful career.

2. Elon Musk:

Elon Musk dedicates himself to ambitious ventures like SpaceX and Tesla but emphasizes the importance of work-life balance and quality family time.

Profiles of Dedicated Individuals and Their Journeys

We delve into the inspiring stories of individuals who exemplify dedication in various aspects of life. These profiles illuminate how unwavering commitment can shape remarkable journeys and lead to extraordinary achievements.

1. **Marie Curie:** The Dedication to Scientific Discovery

Marie Curie's tireless dedication to scientific research on radioactivity earned her two Nobel

Prizes and paved the way for significant scientific advancements.

2. **Serena Williams**: The Dedication to Excellence

Serena Williams' rigorous training, discipline, and perseverance in tennis have made her one of the most successful athletes in history, with numerous Grand Slam titles.

3. **Greta Thunberg:** The Dedication to Environmental Activism

Greta Thunberg's commitment to climate activism has inspired a global movement, raising awareness about climate change and inspiring young activists worldwide.

These profiles offer insights into individuals who have harnessed dedication to drive change, achieve excellence, and leave a lasting impact in their fields. Their journeys serve as beacons of inspiration, reminding us of the transformative power of dedication in our pursuits and aspirations.

Action Steps from The Millionaire Maker, Loral Langemeier for Dedication

When you think of dedication and what it is, I would have you think of dedication as loyalty to yourself and values. Dedication is commitment and continuing on your path even in the toughest of times.

Knowing your core values and knowing your mission will help you stay loyal and dedicated to the goal you are trying to accomplish. You have to announce it, which I call "Living Out Loud", and tell people what you're dedicated to, what you're committed to, and what you want to accomplish.

If you are truly serious about becoming successful, you will want to find three to five people who are dedicated to you just as you will be dedicated to them. This is a Mastermind. Think of it as a group of people coming together for the support and loyalty of one another, to hold everyone accountable and help keep everyone moving forward. The dedication to each other's goal through a mastermind is extraordinary for success and support.

*To Access Book Bonuses, go to: **www.DoYouWantItNow.com**

Action Step: Who am I most DEDICATED to?

_____
_____
_____
_____
_____
_____
_____
_____
_____
_____
_____

Action Step: What are my core values?

_____
_____
_____
_____

Action Step: Today I am choosing to stay committed to:

_____
_____
_____

FUELED BY DESIRE

PSALM 37:4

CHAPTER

Chapter 5

Fueled by Desire

Psalm 37:4

> *Take delight in the Lord, and he will give you the desires of your heart.*

In this final part of our journey, we explore the fifth and pivotal element of success: desire. While discipline, drive, determination, and dedication have laid the foundation, the desire propels us to reach new heights, conquer challenges, and transform our dreams into reality.

The Essence of Desire

Desire is the flame that ignites your passion, fuels your ambition, and drives your pursuit of success. It is the unwavering belief in your goals and an unquenchable thirst to achieve them.

Understanding the Power of Desire

- **Passion and Purpose:** Desire is closely linked to your passion and sense of purpose. It keeps you awake at night, stirs your soul, and gives your goals meaning.

- **Intrinsic Motivation:** Unlike external motivators, desire stems from within— the intrinsic yearning to excel and accomplish what matters most to you.

Cultivating and Harnessing Desire

- **Clarify Your Objectives:** To fuel your desire, it's crucial to have clear and specific goals. Understand what you want to achieve and why it matters deeply to you.

- **Visualize Your Success:** Use the power of visualization to imagine yourself achieving your goals vividly. This mental imagery strengthens your desire by making success feel tangible.

- **Stoke Your Passion:** Regularly engage in activities related to your goals that ignite your passion. Immersing yourself in your pursuits reinforces your desire to excel.

Desire in Action: Real-Life Examples

- **Walt Disney:** Walt Disney's relentless desire to create a place where families could enjoy magical moments led to the creation of Disneyland and Disney World. His unwavering belief in his vision drove him to overcome financial challenges and setbacks.

- **Oprah Winfrey:** Oprah Winfrey's desire to empower and inspire others through media transformed her from a local news anchor to a global media mogul. Her unyielding passion for storytelling and self-improvement continues to drive her success.

- **Muhammad Ali:** Muhammad Ali's desire to be the greatest boxer in history was fueled by unwavering self-belief and an unshakable work ethic. His dedication to his craft and fierce desire for victory made him iconic in sports history.

Overcoming Obstacles with Desire

- **Resilience in the Face of Setbacks:** When setbacks occur, your desire helps you bounce back with determination. Your unwavering belief in your goals fuels your resilience.

- **Adaptation and Flexibility:** Desire also drives your ability to adapt to changing circumstances. Your commitment to your goals empowers you to find new paths when obstacles arise.

The Harmonious

Dance of the Five D's

As we conclude this journey through the Five Ds of success – Discipline, Drive, Determination, Dedication, and Desire – remember that the harmonious integration of these elements unlocks the full potential of your pursuits. Each "D" complements and strengthens the others, creating a symphony of excellence in your life.

By mastering discipline, nurturing drive, summoning determination, cultivating dedication, and being fueled by an unyielding desire, you possess the keys to unlock success in any endeavor. As you move forward, may your journey be marked by passion, purpose, and a resolute commitment to your dreams, propelling you toward the fulfillment of your greatest aspirations.

The Power of Desire in Goal Setting

Desire is the heart of meaningful goal setting. It fuels your ambitions, ignites your inner fire, and instills unwavering belief in your ability to achieve dreams. In this chapter, we explore how desire drives the pursuit of genuinely significant goals.

- **Emotional Resonance:** Desire adds emotional significance to your goals, turning aspirations into passionate pursuits.

- **Sustained Motivation:** Desire is the wellspring of motivation, keeping you committed even in the face of challenges.

The Anatomy of Desire-Driven Goals

- **Clarity and Specificity**: Desire-driven goals are clear and specific, guiding you on a well-defined path.

- **Resilience in Obstacles:** Such goals are more resilient; deep desire propels you to persevere through adversity.

Cultivating Desire in Goal Setting

- **Soul-Searching:** Reflect on your passions and values, aligning your goals with what truly matters to you.

- **Visualization Techniques:** Vividly visualize achieving your goals, reinforcing desire and making success feel attainable.

Overcoming Common Roadblocks

- **Fear and Self-Doubt:** Desire empowers you to conquer inner obstacles like fear and self-doubt.

- **External Influences:** Listen to your heart, setting goals aligned with your authentic desires, not external pressures.

Desire in Action: A Real-Life Example

- **Martin Luther King Jr.:** His desire for racial equality drove the civil rights movement, inspiring transformative change.

The Art of Balancing Desire with Realism

Striking the Balance: Balance desire with realistic planning and action for a potent goal-achieving combination.

Techniques for Maintaining Focus on Your Desires

Desires are powerful motivators, but life's distractions can challenge our focus. This chapter explores techniques to help you stay laser-focused on your desires, ensuring your goals take center stage in your journey.

- **Goal Visualization:** Visualize your desires as if they've been achieved, making mental images vivid and emotional.

- **Goal Setting and Planning:** Break desires into actionable goals, creating a structured roadmap.

- **Affirmations:** Use positive affirmations to reinforce your desires daily.

- **Goal Journaling:** Keep a dedicated journal for aspirations, progress, and obstacles.

- **Accountability Partners:** Share goals with a trusted friend or mentor for support and accountability.

- **Daily Mindfulness Practice:** Incorporate mindfulness into your routine to reduce distractions.

- **Prioritization:** Allocate time and energy to tasks aligning with your desires.

- **Elimination of Distractions:** Identify and remove distractions from your life.

- **Regular Progress Assessment:** Periodically review progress and adapt to changes.

- **Visualization Boards or Vision Boards:** Create visual representations of your desires for daily reminders.

- **Positive Environment:** Surround yourself with supportive individuals who share your aspirations.

- **Self-Reflection:** Understand your motivations and reasons behind your desires.

- **Resilience Building:** Develop resilience to overcome setbacks and challenges.

Transforming Desire into Action: Strategies for Success

Desire is a potent force whose potential soars when directed into actionable steps. Let's delve into techniques to translate your burning desires into concrete actions that propel you closer to your goals.

- **Break It Down:** Divide your overarching desire into smaller, actionable steps. This creates a clear roadmap, making your aspirations feel attainable.

- **Set SMART Goals:** Frame your desires as Specific, Measurable, Achievable, Relevant, and Time-bound (SMART) goals. This approach makes them actionable and manageable.

- **Prioritize Your Steps:** Not all steps hold equal weight. Focus on high-priority tasks that closely align with your desires for maximum impact.

- **Create a Timeline:** Assign deadlines to your actionable steps, infusing urgency into your goals and ensuring you stay on course.

- **Start Small:** Initiate with manageable actions, especially if your desire seems overwhelming. Small successes breed confidence and build momentum.

- **Develop a Plan:** Craft detailed plans for each step, specifying required resources, time, and effort. A well-defined plan minimizes uncertainty and bolsters commitment.

- **Establish Milestones:** Break your journey into milestones and celebrate each achievement. These victories fuel your desire for the next phase.

- **Stay Accountable:** Share your plan with an accountability partner who can help you stay committed through regular check-ins.

Desire initiates action, but actionable steps transform dreams into reality. You empower yourself to channel your deepest aspirations into meaningful achievements by breaking down desires into manageable, time-bound actions. Remember, the journey, fueled by desire and guided by actionable steps, is a remarkable and fulfilling experience.

The Power of Unwavering Desire

We will explore inspiring stories of individuals who achieved remarkable success through their unwavering desire and determination.

Thomas Edison: Lighting the World

Edison's relentless desire to bring light to the world led to the invention of the light bulb, despite thousands of failures.

Steve Jobs: Revolutionizing Technology

Jobs' relentless desire to create innovative technology products transformed industries and changed how we live through Apple.

Mother Teresa: Serving the Destitute

Mother Teresa's unwavering desire to help the destitute earned her global recognition and the Nobel Peace Prize.

Mahatma Gandhi: Champion of Nonviolence

Gandhi's resolute desire for freedom and justice in India led to its independence from British rule through nonviolent resistance.

Your Path to Mastery

Embarking on the journey to master these five words - Discipline, Dedication, Drive, Determination, and Desire - means embracing continuous growth and self-improvement. These words are not mere concepts but dynamic forces propelling you toward your goals.

Mastering these words means not just achieving your goals but surpassing them. Embrace discipline to stay on course, dedication to your purpose, drive to excel, determination to overcome challenges, and the desire that fuels every step.

With this blueprint, you can unlock your full potential and turn aspirations into remarkable achievements.

Success isn't a distant destination; it's the ongoing pursuit of mastering these five powerful words.

This blueprint, forged from Discipline, Drive, Determination, Dedication, and Desire, empowers you to walk in your power and transform your life.

In a world where success may seem reserved for a select few, remember that success is not a secret or a mystery; it's a choice. It's choosing to take action, excel, and leave a lasting legacy.

As you embark on this transformative journey, ask yourself: What legacy do you wish to leave? What words do you want to be remembered for? The blueprint is in your hands, and the power to change your life is within your grasp.

As evident in the trail of success, a common thread binds many achievers: they embrace the power of the 5 D's. It's a proven path to greatness. Will you be among them?

Action Steps from The Millionaire Maker, Loral Langemeier for Desire

Desire is an intrinsic motivation and it's something that you can't get or take from someone else. Just like motivation comes within yourself, desire is something that will require some internal reflection if you want to harness it for your success. I like to use a tool I made up called, Gap Analysis to help people harness that desire accordingly. A gap analysis is understanding exactly where you are, what you want, and then identifying the gap between those two states of reality or being. I use it with my private clients to put a financial baseline together and it helps them determine what their next course of action should be.

That gap between where you are and what you want will usually be your prime motivating factor. Conversely, when I work with people who are not successful or are not reaching their goals, it is usually because they have not yet identified their gaps or set the right goals. I want you to set very realistic goals or what people call, "SMART goals". When you set the right goals based on where you are and what you want, you'll be surprised how the desire to get up, stay determined, stay dedicated, and stay disciplined will rise in your life.

*To Access Book Bonuses, go to: **www.DoYouWantItNow.com**

Action Step: What are my DESIRES?

_____
_____
_____
_____
_____
_____
_____
_____
_____
_____
_____
_____
_____
_____
_____

Action Step: Where do I want to be in a month from now?

_____
_____

Where do I want to be in a year from now?

_____
_____

Where do I want to be 5 years from now?

_____
_____

Conclusion

In my book, 'Do You Want It?', I emphasize the importance of discipline, dedication, drive, determination, and desire as the keys to success. I draw inspiration from the Bible, a collection of 66 different books written by over 40 authors in various parts of the world, who often didn't know each other. Yet, their combined efforts produced the greatest book of all time. This serves as a reminder that success leaves trails. The champions I highlight in my book have achieved greatness in their own right.

They didn't collaborate or plan together, but they all embody these principles. My message is clear: if you apply these words and take action, you too can achieve success and inspire others to do the same. It's about answering your calling, overcoming obstacles, and changing the world.

About The Author

As a devoted husband, father, and fishing enthusiast, I find joy in the simple moments of life. Celebrating five years of sobriety since December 25th, 2019, I embrace each day with gratitude and resilience.

Surviving cancer has fueled my passion for living fully, alongside my love for animals and commitment to physical wellness through swimming, cycling, and running. Twice completing the Hawaii Ironman, I understand the power of perseverance and the mantra,

"I GET TO."

Beyond these endeavors, I am a God-driven action coach, Emmy Award-winning actor known for my role as Lt. Taggert on ABC's General Hospital, and a certified mental wellness coach. My journey includes accomplishments as a seven-figure income earner, author, songwriter, producer, and podcaster, drawing on 37 years of expertise in fitness and mental wellness advocacy.

Through my podcast, "Getting Real with Réal," I strive to inspire and empower others to believe in themselves, echoing my guiding principle: "I will believe in you until you believe in yourself."

Follow, connect, or learn more from Réal here:

www.realandrews.com

https://www.facebook.com/CoachRealAndrews

https://www.instagram.com/realandrews/

https://twitter.com/realandrews

https://www.tiktok.com/@realandrews

*To Access Book Bonuses, go to: **www.DoYouWantItNow.com**

Made in the USA
Columbia, SC
13 April 2024

8d2f1485-96b6-4459-ab13-6b0d9fbe3529R01